ROMAN ARCHITECTURE

THE GREAT AGES OF WORLD ARCHITECTURE

GREEK   *Robert L. Scranton*
ROMAN   *Frank E. Brown*
EARLY CHRISTIAN AND BYZANTINE   *William L. MacDonald*
MEDIEVAL   *Howard Saalman*
GOTHIC   *Robert Branner*
RENAISSANCE   *Bates Lowry*
BAROQUE AND ROCOCO   *Henry A. Millon*
MODERN   *Vincent Scully, Jr.*
WESTERN ISLAMIC   *John D. Hoag*
PRE-COLUMBIAN   *Donald Robertson*
CHINESE AND INDIAN   *Nelson I. Wu*
JAPANESE   *William Alex*

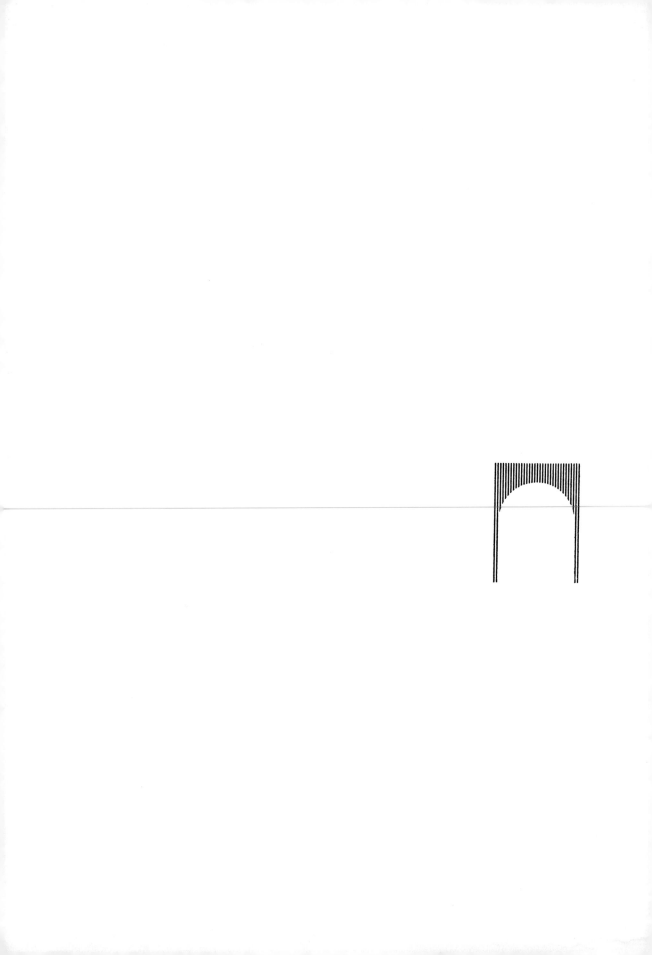

ROMAN ARCHITECTURE

by Frank E. Brown

GEORGE BRAZILLER · NEW YORK

All Rights Reserved
For information address the publisher,
George Braziller, Inc.
Number One Park Avenue
New York, N. Y. 10016

Library of Congress Catalog Card Number: 61-13688
ISBN 0–8076–0331–7
Ninth Printing, 1982

Printed in the United States of America

CONTENTS

Text

1 RITUAL AND SPACE

800–600 B.C.

The architecture of the Romans was, from first to last, an art of shaping space around ritual. It stemmed directly from the Roman propensity to transform the raw stuff of experience and behavior into rituals, formal patterns of action and re-action. From the dawn of their history we find the Romans feeling, thinking, and acting ritually. Together or singly, they sought identity and fulfillment in the performance and creation of fixed, habitual forms of conduct. This was the inherently Roman way of reducing the chaos of experience to manage-able, human measures. It was the root of Roman custom, Roman tradition, Roman discipline, and Roman law. It was in the form of ritual that the specifically Roman values mani-fested themselves.

Ritual is an art of action, but to the Romans it implied an art of another sort—architecture. The form of ritual is a fleeting form, embodied in the act itself or stamped on the nervous system of the agent. But for the Romans it had the power to engender architectural form by the mere fact that it took place in space. Space was informed by ritual. As ritual refined out of crude experience the significant formal pattern, so out of undifferentiated space the significant conformation was precipitated. A particular segment of space took shape from the formal action that occurred in it. It became a capsule, which would reshape itself whenever the ritual was repeated. This spatial form, belonging to a given ritual and established by repetition, acquired independent, architectural existence. It could be framed separately and at will for the express purpose of the intended ritual. Such a shape of space was architecture, even though immaterial. It was architecture of a peculiarly functional sort. Of its very nature, it not only contained the specific action it was framed for; it required it, prompted it, enforced it.

The great rituals of the earliest Romans were those of the cultivation of the gods, the life of the family, and the ordering of the community. Each begot a conformation of space to suit it. Man's control over his environment was exercised through these discrete units of formal action and space, hewn out of the wilderness of phenomena. The first Roman architects were, no doubt, the priestly leaders who prayed, made sacrifice, and asked the gods for signs. For these rituals of worship they framed the appropriate spaces. Construction was by incantation. It was enough to declare: "this space shall be for worship and for nothing else; it shall be four-square; its boundaries shall be this, that and the other; whatever is done or said in this holy space the gods shall be aware of; whatever comes into this holy space from above shall be a sign from the gods." The enclosure of space was complete and rigid, although invisible and impalpable. Its inner configuration was fixed by the ritual act. The worshiper, standing at the middle or at one end, facing in the right direction, established front and back, right side and left side, center, axis, and cross-axis, gave the "temple" its symmetry of lines of force, which admitted no deviation.

The first tangible Roman buildings were the huts that housed the life of the family and symbolized the individual's absorption in it even after death. Their traces in the ground and the miniature models that served for burial (Plate 1) show us rough structures of post, wattle, daub, and thatch, barely adequate to shelter family and fire from the weather. The oval outline, the helmet of roof with its ridge on the transverse axis, the doorway at one vertex, sometimes a porch, and a central post or hearth describe a compactly symmetrical mass with a single sweep and approach, a symmetrical volume traversed by a dominant axis. So far the rudimentary means and skills of the builder could frame a space to match the ingrained patterns of conduct and obligation under the absolute rule of the father.

The architecture of the primitive Roman community as a whole bears witness to the same disparity between envisioned space and its embodiment in structure. The open space where the village fathers met was no physical counterpart of the sharply defined and solemnly inaugurated precinct of the mind, within which alone they could perform the ritual of deliberation and come to binding decisions. The ditch and earthen mound, which fenced the commonwealth from the unreclaimed tracts and men outside, had less reality and virtue than the magic barrier that imagination drew about the village. The gaps in the mound, by which one passed from one world to the other, were merely symbols of the architecture that the rituals of leaving, approaching, and entering erected as the goals of movement and sight for the inner eye.

The earliest Romans were congenitally disposed to be architects. They were ready with the designs of the spaces to fit and foster the rituals they lived by. They had to be taught to build them lastingly of solid materials that would take the shapes of their vision.

2 OLD ROME

600–200 B.C.

The Romans learned the art of building along with many other things from their neighbors and overlords, the Etruscans. Something, too, they may have learned more directly from the teachers of the Etruscans, the Greeks of that day, who were reaching into Italy with bands of colonists and free-roving traders and artisans. At their first lessons the Romans were apt and docile pupils, copying faithfully what they were taught. As they had learned from Etruscans or Greeks to entertain images of their gods, so they learned to make a house for the image, to hide it from ordinary sight and protect it from the weather. Long, prismatic boxes of stone, crude brick, timber, and tile, their like might be found almost anywhere in Etruria, in the Greek colonies of South Italy and Sicily, or in

Greece itself. Huts were converted into more permanent dwellings after the same model. The ellipse was squared to a gable-ended oblong. Anterooms or annexes were added. At Rome the ancient king's house of this time was preserved out of awe and custom, and rebuilt over and over again in its original aspect (Plate 2). A hall with central hearth was preceded by two antechambers. Beside it lay a walled courtyard with storage pit and well.

These elementary lessons were soon digested, the basic techniques and forms soon assimilated. By the end of the sixth century Rome had expelled the Etruscan kings who had made it a city. The Romans were now self-governed, and Roman architects could begin to give enduring shape to the spaces their institutions called for. The fifth, fourth, and third centuries B.C. saw that steady gush of creative energy that made Rome's heroic age. It forged and tempered the uniquely Roman patterns of ritual action in war and peace. It forged and tempered at the same time their spatial environment of architecture. The result was an autonomous and independent art, unlike that of any other part of the contemporary world. We may call it "Old Roman." It had its own vision of the measure of man in space. It had unmistakable formal identity, its own canons of scale and proportion, its own uses for mass and color, its own repertory of buildings and decoration. Through and through it was an architecture framed to hold men's actions in its grip, to remind them of—and steer them in—the right way of doing things.

The ritual of public worship henceforward took place in the presence of the god's image sheltered in its house. The true "temple" was, as before, the open space where, about the altar, the strictly stylized act of offering and prayer was performed. This space was sometimes outlined as a terrace, by means of a curbing or parapet. It was generated and fixed in its limits by the house of the image (Plates 3–5). The holy house created the Old Roman temple by being in it or on it, by standing at the back of the area it overshadowed and converted to the sacred purpose. It was raised high on a podium, accessible only from the front. Its overhanging eaves and beetling gable reached out and down to define the volume of the tight space where the worshiper stood and to assert their control throughout it. The mass of the building commanded the worshiper's attention, his attitude, and his movement by its firm axial dominance. The broad, upward sweep of the stair, the heavy horizontals of the façade, its convergence by spacing and decoration upon the center drew and riveted mind and body to the ritual act. Color, from the dun footing of the temple space to the clear die of walls and columns and the bright, ambiguous fretwork of their painted crown of terra cotta, magnified its power. Unlike the Greek temple, which was a prismatic solid isolated in free space, the house of the image was an organic part of the space it generated. The skeletal openness of its forms gathered space between the wide-set columns and beneath the jutting timbers of the roof. A clinging mantle of shadow shifted against the highlighted surfaces, masking their structural consistency and rigidity.

The Old Roman house, the second major achievement of this architecture, took shape as the mold of the complex ritual of Roman family life. It enclosed in a structured envelope a hierarchy of spaces as set and formal as the nexus of traditional ties they represented (Plates 6, 7). The blank exterior of the house was merely the shell of a manifold, rigorously ordered, interior world, which was the matrix of the authority of the father—absolute, patterned, and fixed by usage. Its essential and invariable parts were the broad entrance passage, the skylighted hall with chambers ranked on either side, the confronted alcoves, and the ample drawing room open to the hall. These were tightly organized around the middle space and source of light, in a highly condensed and articulated plan. Its deliberate symmetry and insistent axiality were underscored by the sequence, size, shape, and graduated lighting of its members. They were counterbalanced by the attraction of its luminous center. The clear spatial statement of precedence, the clear shape of before, behind, and beside, and of great and small, both expressed and guided duty, discipline, and decorum.

The shaping of space by polarization and enclosure and the specific forms of temple and house provided the means for singling out, architecturally, certain functions of civic life. Religiously appointed precincts answered to the formal procedure of meetings of the citizen body under the control of the magistrates and to the equally formal procedure of sessions of the permanent council of magistrates. Assembly place and council hall were fashioned together after the example of the temple (Plate 8). The circular Comitium within its ordained square became a shallow bowl of ascending steps, dominated by the looming mass of the Senate House above and behind it. The architect diagramed in a single geometric configuration of space both the theater of equal right and voice, focused on a central concern, and the common approach to vested authority. It was the household that set the pattern of spatial order for everyday public business (Plate 9). Its central unit of volume, which was ample, unbroken, and uniformly lit, made a single vessel suited to the conduct of varied affairs. The great hall of the house, lifted from its domestic context, had, in its severe axial symmetry, a forceful spatial design in which orderly procedure was at home.

The buildings of this Old Roman architecture were conceived as the visible poles or the visible shells of space. The power to shape space was exerted by their surfaces, outer or inner. The fabric that supported these surfaces was in itself indifferent, save as it governed the architectural conception or limited its realization. The Old Roman architects had come to have at their command the materials at hand and the skills of working them. They used the dark, soft stone of the volcanic regions of Central Italy and the hard, grey limestone of the Apennines, which gave them also the fine lime for their mortars and plasters. They used the fat, local clays for brick and terra cotta, and the timber in which the country abounded. They knew how to handle the stone by itself or with clay or lime as rubblework of broken stone and mortar—a versatile material, capable of adaptation to a wide range of forms. They knew how to use each kind of timber boldly, in its proper place, to trust it, and to protect it from the weather. Yet these building materials and the structural system of vertical support and horizontal load were of little account architecturally, since they evoked no necessary visible expression. It was on the dynamic surfaces of mass or volume that the architect spent his effort and depended for his effect. Hence, while stonework might be profiled, jointed, or finished to be seen for its own value, it might equally well, like walling of brick or rubblework, be hidden by stucco, trimmed or painted. Hence the visible surfaces of timber might be carved, painted, or sheathed with plates of terra cotta.

Old Roman architecture also possessed the means to shape more broadly the whole environment of urban life, in so far as it had crystallized in patterns of common situations, mastered by forms of customary action. It could make manifest the staunchness of the invisible, sacred boundary of the community in walls of massive stone (Plates 10, 11). Their surfaces were wrought to display the elemental strength and refractory shape of the living rock, disciplined by the civilized will. It could embody in deep gateways the potent significance of passage and prospect. It could impose on all within them a general conformation, which regulated the relations of its separate parts and activities (Plate 12). Temples, dwellings, civic center, worship, household, and self-government were meshed together in a formal pattern of flow and visual focus, established by a systematic network of streets. These conduits of habitual action—aimed at the primary objectives of daily life, functionally graded in size, and rigorously rectilinear—completed the architectural definition of living space.

The Old Roman way of life and architecture was insular in the world of that time, remote from the lively currents of Classical and Early Hellenistic Greece. It was the way of a closed world, bounded by the Roman horizon, containing in itself both its ideals and the means of attaining them. This horizon had been gradually stretched to encompass almost the whole peninsula of Italy, but the world within it was still one, a single domain of inveterate stereotypes of behavior and form.

Their adequacy to cope with every contingency within the domain whose order they constituted had been triumphantly demonstrated. In the Hellenistic world outside, men's minds were divided, their loyalties compromised, and their purposes unsure. Now, in the latter half of the third century B.C., when the two worlds came to their unavoidable collision, the issue was not in doubt. The unshakable confidence and unflinching discipline of the Roman world rode roughshod over all in its path. In less than a century the horizon of Rome had been dramatically lifted and their world enlarged by the Romans themselves.

3   HELLENISTIC ROME

200–50 B.C.

The opening of the world to Rome by conquest, power, and wealth was the beginning of a revolutionary phase in which Roman architecture was remade. As radical and sweeping as the Renaissance in Europe, it had many of the traits of that more familiar time. It was the bursting of a traditional order of things through the liberation of forces until then dormant and confined within a customary round. It was sparked by the confrontation of the inherited order with an older, richer, freer order, the order of Greece. Architecture was swept up during the course of the third century in the greater revolution of Roman perception and thought. This was a rebirth, a coming alive to a world of seemingly limitless possibilities, a world beyond the tight, old order of values and spaces. Greece was the inspiring teacher, the initiant into stirring mysteries of experience and sensibility, of meaning, and form. Greece, "taking the brutish conqueror captive," aroused and set him momentarily free.

That moment was a moment of self-discovery and self-awareness. In the dazzling light of Greek reason the old rituals were no longer self-evident. New, unwonted situations crowded in. The old had to be justified, discarded, or recast. The new had to be met and, because by Romans, not merely by recognition but by action. The moment of self-criticism was also a moment of self-assurance. The new experience was stubbornly digested into ritual. This making and remaking of the forms of action was at the same time a making and remaking of the forms of space. The moment called for the rebuilding of Rome in the new image of itself and for an enlarged way of life in rivalry with a greater world. For this, the light of reason was the light of Hellenistic Greek architecture.

Hellenistic architecture held out an example of mannered elegance and experimental freedom. It challenged Roman architects to new appetites and sensibilities, prompted a buoyant phase of hungry assimilation and restless creativity. On the one hand, it was a model. Hellenistic architecture made the Roman eye and mind dissatisfied with the traditional shapes and proportions of mass—broad, squarish, and top-heavy. It taught them to share its own predilection for the oblong, the tall, and lightly loaded. On the other hand, it was a goad. Hellenistic architects had invented the timber truss, using it timidly here and there for special purposes. The Romans appropriated it as a device for producing great, uninterrupted volumes and turned it to their own uses. Again, Hellenistic architecture, through contact with the Orient, had experimented gingerly with the arch and barrel vault, never to define a significant form or volume but as a variant of opening or passage. Roman architects were moved to seize on the arch as the formal substitute for post and lintel, and on the vault as the means of closing the shell of space in a continuous curve. In the heat of building, under the spur of their new incentives, they perfected old materials and invented new methods. From rubblework came concrete, laid between masonry forms, which yielded its permanent faces. The plastic wall with the help of centering became the complete plastic shell.

The old architecture had laid down the basic configuration of the Roman temple once and for all. The rituals of public worship were the least liable to be affected by the new atmosphere. Yet the house of the image was stripped of much of its generative power over the space before it by the new sensibility, which shaped its mass. The borrowed mass and surface syntax of the Hellenistic temple building held it aloof—the more for being planted on a Roman podium—from the area at its feet (Plate 13). The loss was made good by another borrowing from the East, the enveloping colonnade. The Greeks used it as a spacious backdrop and frame of reference. The architects of Hellenistic Rome drew it tightly about the temple space to second the frontal façade by cloistering the sacred proceedings and by accompanying them with the rhythmic iteration of its columns (Plates 14, 15). The holy place might be even more dramatically detached from its surroundings by being lifted above them on a soaring substructure of arches and vaults (Plate 16).

Greece, like the Orient, had been shy of the curve in plan. Yet Greece had accepted the semicircular auditorium and had created a circular building, the tholos. These by-forms became at the hands of Roman architects—not unpracticed, as their old assembly places show—the essentials of a new idiom. Element by element the rectilinear determinants of space were bent to curves. The house of the image might become a rotunda (Plate 17), the recess an apse, the approach a theatral semicircle—in a mounting tension of curved and straight, axial and centrifugal lines of force. At Praeneste (Plates 18–20) they were spectacularly combined in a manifold scheme in which ceremonial discipline controlled vision and movement in hitherto unexampled ways. There, the processional ritual of a great oracular sanctuary moved punctiliously up a hillside to the revelation of the rotunda at the top. It was set in an intricate choreography of space. In it the architect, like a ballet master, marked with inflexible symmetry the figures, the steps, and the tempo. His measures were the flow of vaults,—ramping, annular, coupled—the punctuation of arches, and the ripple of columns. In the convergent, tunnel-like ramps and the divergent, contrasted terraces its cadences were balanced and stressed. In rhythmic repetitions and alternations of centrifugal and centripetal focus, through the axial surges of stairs, the stately temple square, and the tensely addorsed curves of approach and rotunda—it swept to a climax.

The house had been the faithful likeness of the old institutions of the Roman family. Its old forms remained for public display as the conventional portrait of a changed reality. The loosing of the strict bonds that had knotted the individual freed him to a private life of a new sort, an expansive life of personal choice and cultivation. Its spatial counterpart was not to be found in the stiff, formal mold of the traditional house. It was added behind the façade of the old, a relaxed expanse of open garden, about which varied new units of living space were arbitrarily disposed (Plate 21). The shapes of the old style, which now were the public antechambers to this spacious privacy, were majestically redesigned to serve their primarily representational function (Plate 22). The outer portal opened to a studiously framed inner façade at the back of the voluminous hall, which was traversed by the enfilade through its light-bathed center and the shadowed drawing room to the bright release beyond. Progress along the line of sight was forced to skirt the center with its pool, now often hemmed by columns, dissolving the fixed vista and opening in succession the ample measures of the room. The inner life about the garden was also governed by laws of motion and vision that were not less binding because capricious. Its overruling harmony was stated by the screen of columns about the open space (Plate 23). However, this admitted, in calculated variations of its spacing to emphasize axes and to frame targets of attention, the will of a personality to impose the single view and the single approach. Each individual space behind it—

dining room, sitting room, library, picture gallery (Plate 24)–
was shaped as willfully and as decisively to its particular function in a life of multiform refinement.

It was this age also that discovered the countryside as the
scene of the fullest life of the freed and cultivated Roman, a
stage to be set by his contrived view of it. The theater of this
life, in but not of the landscape, was the villa (Plates 25, 26). It
was lifted cleanly out of its surroundings, a compact and alien
body on an artificial platform. Its interior conformation brought
the essence of urbanity to the country, repeating the symmetrical cocoon of conventional private life in town with its full
gamut of imperatives and involvements, its enfilades, and
enveloping spaces. But life in the country looked outward as
well, through the eyes of the villa. Its shell was pierced by view-
finding apertures. Its outer rooms were turned upon framed
prospects. From its height it directed the outlook of its owner
as firmly as it did the motions of his daily life, sorting vistas
out of the field of vision, and cutting the spread of landscape
into significant segments.

In the larger context of affairs more unprecedented demands
were made on the Roman capacity to give definitive form to
action and space. The public life of Hellenistic Rome had in-
creased and diversified itself in step with the Roman world.
The old, formulaic spaces could no longer contain it. The time
called for an order of space capacious and adaptable to various
transactions to the exclusion of others; one able to confer on
those it was meant to accommodate their due consequence and
dignity, and to propagate its own order. Roman architects
answered with the basilica. Conceived under the inspiration of
the aisled and storied porticoes of the Hellenistic East, made
possible by the timber truss, it was a new thing under the sun–
a lucid box of undivided volume, surrounded by a continuous,
shadowed corridor (Plates 27–29). A columnar skeleton provided clerestory lighting in the central vessel and screened off
the aisles. The ample nave was to be grasped as a single whole,
clearly scanned by the intervals of its framing. It placed men
at its center or drew them to move lengthwise or crosswise of

22

it. The ambulatory unfolded progressively with movement along it or subdivided itself in the stationary units of its bays. Within it special spaces of arrest might be signaled by tribunes, or alcoves or windows, placed in axial relation to the whole. The two orders of space were functionally discrete yet complementary, contrasted in scale, and unified by a common module. The same columnar module determined the exterior aspect, imposing the basilica's inner discipline on the space before it.

Many another archetype of public building had its origin in the hotbed of Hellenistic Rome—theater, amphitheater, and monumental avenue among the rest. Of most of them the vehicles and instruments of structural and spatial invention were the arch and the vault. The pressing, workaday needs of the economy of a new world-capital, and the uses of a new refinement were met by bold experiment with vaulted spaces. The functional clarity and simplicity of these designs, the confident skill with which they were carried out, are nowhere better evidenced than in the great Tiber-side warehouse that was among the earliest (Plates 30, 31). Fifty stepped barrel vaults, carried on files of arches, made parallel halls lit from before, behind, and above in clerestory fashion. The arcades opened them to each other in ranks of galleries, running the length of the building. Here, space was forthrightly organized, and both lit and ventilated for specific activities in a firm, uncluttered texture.

In the same spirit similar solutions were found for the more intricate functional and spatial problems presented by the new rite of public ablutions. Affluence and well-being had generalized the practice of leisurely care of the body and had given it a pattern of exercise and bathing, which took the form we know as the Turkish bath. As a fixed, public institution it gave rise to an order of spaces answering not only to its ritual program but also to its requirements of dressing and undressing, a supply of hot and cold water, variably controlled temperature, and separation of sexes. Apart from the exercise grounds and the requisite installations of radiant heating through floors and walls, furnaces, boilers, and plumbing, these earliest solutions of Roman architects were based on the use of barrel vaults in series (Plates 32, 33). Spaces of sizes sorted with their functions were ranked across the line of the fixed sequence of bathing from cool to hot and back again. Their axes at right angles to the progressive movement were established by apses, pools, basins, and windows. Staggered doorways and varied surfaces made each a distinct moment in a chain of separate experiences. Each took place in a cylindrical capsule. The vaults, springing at radius height, and hovering over the participant, had the effect of closing the circle of space about him, restrained only by the flatness of the floor, and the verticality of the walls.

Of the exuberant productivity of the age these buildings are a thin sample, but they have survived to testify to its protean creativity and to its seminal potency for the future. That future was now at hand. By the middle of the first century before our era the revolutionary phase was over. The Romans had gathered up what they might of the physical and spiritual inheritance of the ancient world and had made it their own. The old, insular Rome was gone, except as a venerable exemplar. Greece was no longer a presence but a past, no longer an incitement but a standard—the classic. Out of the double past had come the triumphant synthesis that was the Roman Empire.

4   THE EARLY EMPIRE

50 B.C.–50 A.D.

The Roman Empire, like Old Rome, was above all else a moral order of values and attitudes emanating from Rome and prevalent in the lands that looked to Rome as the capital. It was an order realized in institutions and practices, that governed men's thoughts and actions as far as the Empire reached. It was a human order, justified by the inherent nature of man and his universe, an order in which Greek speculation became the Roman reality. The latter half of the first century before our era established the Empire as the mode of peace and welfare. The following century promoted and propagated it in humane and efficacious rituals of universal relevance. The architecture of the Empire, since it was Roman architecture, was an order of spaces shaped to constitute the environment of its moral order, matching its security and dignity with decorous spatial grandeur. It, too, was an emanation from the capital, coterminous with its horizon. Architecture, over the length and breadth of the Empire, embodied and inculcated its dispensation, and solicited obedience to its rituals.

The architecture of the first century of the Empire had emerged from the Hellenistic adventure to a soberer mood and heavier responsibilities. Its new task was nothing less than to interpret unmistakably to all the meaning of the Empire in forms as lasting as they were impressive. For this, architecture relied upon what, among the achievements of the last generation, approved itself as solid, sure, and firmly anchored in the double past, rejecting its more radical innovations. To practiced competence in the handling of masonry, concrete and timber, arches, vaults and trusses, it could now add a richer variety of surfaces. The fact of empire made available to Roman architects inexhaustible supplies of hard, crystalline stone, the marbles, granites, and porphyries of the whole Mediterranean basin. To the elements of mass or to the revetment of the plastic wall these brought the highly sculptured form, the mat or polished finishes, and the wide register of colors with which the architect manipulated shadow and reflected light.

The gods, to whom the Empire addressed its rituals of public worship, had become the symbols of the forces that had brought the Empire to pass, animated it, and would maintain it. They stood for the traditions and institutions whose historically accumulated power was so much greater than the capacity of any generation of men, any emperor, good, bad, or indifferent, to add or detract. They were the eternal witnesses and guarantors of the rightness and expediency of Rome's self-destined supremacy. Now, as never before, the gods were identified with the state. Now, as never before, the due performance of secular rituals was a form of worship and due worship an official act. Now, as never before, the temple stood for the Empire. Its traditional forms—high podium, deep porch, dominant façade—now generalized, transmitted unaltered the power of the house of the image over the ritual space. Its new dress of gleaming stone and rich chiaroscuro heightened its portentous impact.

The imperial role of the temple affected its design in other ways. The house might now stand alone as temple, sufficient in itself, drawing its altar up into the mass of its stair or platform (Plate 34). It was as though the house had absorbed the temple space or dispersed it, as though the temple space were now as boundless as the Empire or implicit in the official act of the worshiper. Again, the house might unite under its control the combined rituals of worship and of public affairs in a single temple of the sacred and the profane (Plates 35–38). The colonnaded area of the Hellenistic temple was narrowed and drawn out, compressed and focused by columnar screens into a fully closed forecourt, roofed by a determined rectangle of sky. Behind its penetrable envelope, inner colonnades and, behind them, chambers, halls, or apsidal recesses made so many spatially discrete, and functionally specialized rooms. All were subject to the static symmetry of the composition, the dynamic symmetry of its axial vectors, under the dominance of the divine presence. Such was the basic design of the "imperial fora": huge cells of definite and concentrated function, walled off from the irrelevancy of other kinds of human activity, and first carried out in the Forum of Caesar and the Forum of Augustus in Rome. Such was the enduring pattern which, condensed or expanded, the religion of the Empire impressed wherever it came. To the new towns that were building in the West (Plate 39) its forms brought participation in the sacred tradition and the full import of disciplined action in an ordered world. Upon the old sanctuaries of the East, refashioned to this pattern (Plate 40), it set the stamp of Rome, giving the old gods new meaning as symbols of the Empire to which they now belonged.

The architects of the Early Empire had also to give definitive form for the whole Roman world to the archetypal festival spaces of the Roman people. Their Hellenistic predecessors had shown the way. The religiously appointed gatherings of the people to honor or placate the gods and rejoice themselves with processions and displays of prowess had always been an integral part of Roman life. From time immemorial they had been major charges of the state, recurrent public functions, which took their place among the most momentous rituals. At the races, at the games that pitted men against men or men against beasts, and at the musical play or the ballet, the people was assembled, and its voice was heard only less formally than in public meeting. Now, as part of the larger Roman order of the Empire, both the institutions and the spaces to contain them were of no less moment. The heirs to earlier architectural experiment, strong in their technical proficiency, solved systematically the functional problems they confronted by the creation of masses and volumes framed to each specific requirement and fixed in master designs of universal application.

They conceived cups and bowls and troughs of space, so shaped as to funnel the spectator's attention toward each distinct, formal pattern of spectacle, so perforated as to channel the flow of large numbers expeditiously in and out, to and from their assigned places, so presented as to assert the public importance and dignity of the proceedings and to invite penetration to the core of space. The appropriate figure of each spatial concavity was directly reflected in the curved or straight contours of the exterior. Each was supported by an ingenious structural web of radial and concentric vaulted passageways. Each presented to public view tiers of open, enframed arches, so spaced and proportioned as to suggest, from a distance, timeless stability in a continuous, fugitive negation of perspective and, close at hand, irresistible attraction.

The terraced and revetted hillside of the Greek theater with its detached scene-building was transformed into a single, compact, free-standing structure, uniting auditorium and stage. It enfolded a deep semicone of space, converging on the center of the stage, and screened from the extraneous realities of the outside world by a fantastically storied architectural prospect. The sense of the ancient assembly place was not forgotten in its design. The presence of the presiding deity might even now be manifested in a shrine set at the back of the auditorium, to which the seats were the stairs of approach. The solution, perhaps reached a generation earlier in the Theater of Pompey, was complete in the Theater of Marcellus of 13 B.C. in Rome (Plates 41–43). From then on it was applied, early and late, throughout the cities of the Empire (Plates 44, 45).

The Roman contests of men and animals had assumed their settled forms and rules in the rectangle of the public square with the spectators all about it. The Roman architect who must fit a space to the spectacle was given the geometrical problem of approximating equidistance from the rectangular field with a curvilinear equivalent. In the amphitheater (Plates 46–49) he resolved it by the ellipse. The unprecedented design of multifocal bowl and evasively curving shell defied clear definition from a particular viewpoint and gave the amphitheater its peculiar spatial dynamism. The design, along with the cellular structure, was perfected in the same school and at the same time as that of the theater. The amphitheaters of Verona and Puteoli (Plates 46, 47) were among the earliest. The Colosseum at Rome (Plates 48, 49) was the greatest of the scores of such structures that were built up and down the Empire.

The race course and processional track first received comparably monumental treatment in the imperial Circus Maximus at Rome (Plate 50), where it was the most venerable of festival places. The shape it was thenceforward and everywhere to keep had been given it by the rooted conventions of its use. Within its spatial trough the intrinsic symmetry of the traditional layout (Plates 51, 52)—the hairpin track with long stretches, tight turns, and median spine, the axial portals— imposed an over-all form. It was compelling enough to annul the functional asymmetry of the starting end with its oblique arc of starting boxes and canted right wall. The counterclockwise orbit of the spectacle that held the eyes of the onlooker kept his sense of the form from being dissipated by its extreme length. From the ground without, such a hippodrome could make no single impression. It was at best a series of partial visions, related by the continuous flight of its arcades. The architect deliberately laid emphasis on the ends, which might be grasped as wholes, building them about conspicuous central gateways.

The Empire was an empire of cities with a city at its head. Its order was an urban order. The first century of the Empire was a time of the building and rebuilding of cities to further that order. From the raw frontiers to the ancient centers, in the formation of new and the reformation of old cities, the principle of organization was the same. It was the Old Roman conception of the city as a system of discrete, functional enclosures of space, connected by arterial channels. The channels were streets and avenues, and in the architecture of the Empire they came into their own. They came to be felt and treated as independent spatial entities, shaped and articulated to instigate directional movement (Plates 53–55). By means of continuous colonnades or arcades, by means of the regular march of verticals, stretched or linked in flow between convergent horizontals, the street was made a measured tunnel. By means of monumental archways, which spanned it, the street was aimed at its objectives. By means of lateral archways, breaking the rhythm of its colonnades, it was articulated at crossings. The street became a substantive building, a public building with a skylighted, central tube of transit and shadowed aisles, that fell into uniform bays of pause. As such, it assembled the economic life of the city in shops and offices ranked behind its porticoes, subjecting to its spatial laws another of the daily routines of living.

As the Empire by urbanization strove to become an unbroken tissue of townships, each town, reaching out toward its neighbors, laid on its hinterland the pattern of its own man-made urban order. The natural countryside was netted by the orthogonals, roads and balks, of the regular plotting of the farm land (Plate 56). It was dramatically brought to bear on its urban center by the aqueducts that slanted across it (Plate 57). The great conduits that everywhere fed the thirsty towns, carried by their striding arches, ruled across the accidents of landscape unwavering skylines. So the highways, making straight across the flat (Plate 58), slicing through the rough (Plate 59), or lifted over it on bridges or viaducts (Plate 60), wrought the landscape to man's will. By them it was constricted to a single dimension and a single direction, determined by human uses. By them man was urged forward, kept from straying, and brought to his goal. All this, too, was part of the architecture of the Empire, the fixation of space in forms constructed by and for the self-disciplined actions of men.

5   THE HIGH EMPIRE
50–250 A.D.

During the first century of its existence, the Empire, within its elastic and pervious borders, had taken form as an aggregate of such town- and land-scapes. The statesmen and architects of the Early Empire, building solidly upon the past, had realized its potentialities in a more and more homogeneous universe of spatial and spiritual order and security. They had bound it together by highways and by the waterways of its central sea. They had bound it still more tightly by patterns of behavior and thought, and by customary rituals of conduct and observance. They had brought more and more and wider and wider fields of human experience under the discipline of ritual and space, as though every significant moment of life might eventually be clothed in an appropriate pattern of response.

Now, in the maturity of its second and third centuries, the Empire was constituted, a universe confidently shaped by man for self-sufficient man, to embody, as he saw it, the fullness and meaning of a life completely his to order. Its spaces proudly celebrated not only the dignity of his achievement and its universality but also, now, the majesty of the imperial presence, which guided and personified the imperial cosmos. The architects of the High Empire worked not only within the great designs laid down by their masters. They strove to surpass them, to convey both the means of man's endeavor to shape himself and his world and its ends. They sought spaces that would elevate, foster, prompt, and enforce but also describe the goals and their mutability, their dependence on the effort of individual and collective attention and performance.

The architects of the High Empire reworked the old designs with great virtuosity into varied ensembles of fresh power. But, more and more, they turned from them toward complete enclosure of space by curved surfaces. Confident mastery of their materials made them free to throw great vaults over space and swing great curves around it. Experience taught them to conceal structural support in the body of structural fabric. The single aim of molding space led them to model their plastic surfaces boldly and to regard mass as a by-product. The spaces they achieved by these means, though variform, were serenely bubblelike in volume and equilibrium. They were so proportioned as to clasp the activity they enveloped in a calmly finite encirclement, like that of a bell jar. Space, above and at either hand, closed equidistantly about man at the center. It might be distended in apses or niches, or indented by groins or columns. Its wholeness was never dissipated. The confines of volume were made taut and clear or fretted and ambiguous by modeling, perforation, and color. Light from high, in or under the vaults, articulated volume supplely by brilliance and sharp shadow or by the shimmer of reflection and veils of shade.

It was the old designs that continued to give the Empire its great spaces for the conduct of civic affairs. The master plan of the Imperial Fora, which identified the orders of the eternal and the transitory, was the basis of the new designs, which sought to invest still more completely official life in a single spatial composition. The common property of these designs (Plates 61–64) was the closing of the temple space more or less emphatically by the opposed and transverse mass of a basilica. Similar orders of central vessel, uncovered and covered, each encompassed by galleries of continuous, statically diversified space, were juxtaposed cross-axially and more or less fused. The divine symbol of the Empire's dispensation and the place of its daily manifestation in human affairs were majestically balanced off, majestically united by the perfect responsion of their symmetries.

The last of the Imperial Fora, the Forum of Trajan (Plate 61), seems to have given the example, although it was itself atypical. Its forum proper was not a temple space. A vast, open square, end-stopped across its full width by the clifflike mass of the clerestory of its basilica, it was itself brought to focus upon its center. The long axis from the monumental gateway to the middle portal of the basilica and the short axis, intimated by the open hemicycles behind the colonnades at either side, met there in a colossal image of the emperor. The imperial presence, more than human, was the source of the order of the forum as of the order of the Empire. It directed the formal pattern of use, as it generated the pattern of its environment. The forum was the forecourt of the basilica, dominated, though not shaped, by its bulk. The basilica was the covered counterpart of the forum (Plate 62): an augustly luminous volume, doubly wrapped by shadowed galleries, behind which, at the ends, wide apses opened, repeating the hemicycles of the forum. The scrolled memorial column in its courtyard behind the basilica and the temple, appended as an afterthought, lay outside the spatial composition and played no part in forming it.

The complete design was spread over the Empire with many variations of expressive emphasis. At its clearest and most concise it may be seen in such provincial versions as that of Augusta Raurica in Switzerland (Plate 63). There, temple building and basilica faced each other openly. The colonnaded expanse between, unmistakably generated by the one and terminated by the other, was modulated only by the gabled accents of twin gatehouses over a street that traversed it. Lepcis Magna in North Africa, on the other hand, displayed a grander and more disjunctive paraphrase (Plate 64). The ample temple square was a self-contained enclosure within its ranges of arcades. The upper aisle and clerestory of the basilica loomed behind it, shutting it in but visually severed from it. The one visual link was the open concavity of the half-dome of an apsidal portal on the axis of the forum. It rose above the roof of the arcade, anticipating and preparing experience of the open-apsed nave of the basilica within.

It was of the old components of sacred space, the gabled mass and the colonnaded temple space before it, that a great architect made the Pantheon at Rome (Plate 65). In it he celebrated the imperial idea and all the gods of the Empire who stood for it. To do so he placed the worshiper in familiar ritual surroundings and through them led him to the vision of the changeless laws and forces that informed Empire and universe alike. The long, attenuated temple space was totally filled by the masterful spread of the façade (Plate 66), so designed that originally it gave no hint of what lay behind it. Beneath the deep porch, space was channeled in three wide bays, where, in the middle, the overarched reveals and, at either side, half-domed niches introduced the transition to curved form. Within the momentary contraction of the doorway, space opened and swelled to a new dimension (Plates 67, 68).

The form of the house of the image was the form of the cosmos with man at its center. The shape of space was the shape of a perfect circle as the base of a perfect sphere, the circle of the Empire's horizon under the dome of its firmament. It was a space bounded, clear, complete, all-encompassing, having power both to magnify and to diminish. The circle of its base was pierced and fretted with openings and indentations. Its limit was tensely definite but compromised. It was kept unbroken by the sense of the whole. Above, the bound was clean and unambiguous. The whole was filled with radiance from a single source overhead, diffused, save for a moving spot of intenser light that swung about it, bringing part after part to quivering life. It swept in the lower half the richly variegated marbles that gave the envelope its warm colors of earth and life. Above, unchanging, was the single tone of the cloudless hemisphere, uniformly picked out with flecks of light. This geometrical perfection of circle and sphere of space was in every direction imbued with law. It was modulated and articulated by diametrical axes, established by the doorway and the opposite apse, and by the regular alternation and opposition of shadowed bays and highlighted aediculae. It was bound by a firm texture of rectilinear directives in the verticals and horizontals of its paneling, in the compelling order of the coffers above, mirrored in the squares of the pavement.

The interior of the Pantheon portrayed the worshipful make of the imperial universe in a great static abstraction. Because of its ultimate simplicity, it also portrays not only the spatial ideals but, like a laboratory specimen, the building practices of the architects of the High Empire. The immense fabric, apart from its façade, was merely the shell of its interior. It existed solely in virtue of the hollow it surrounded. The huge drum with its saucer of dome was a result, not an end, and had no formal value. The architect studiously masked it from proximate view and gilded the dome to catch the eye enigmatically at the great distances from which it might be perceived. Construction was the modeling of a plastic material on a gigantic scale (Plate 69). The ring of self-buttressing structure was enormously thick and weighty. It was honeycombed at regular intervals by empty shafts, not so much to lighten its bulk or to concentrate its stresses as, by a nice adjustment of surface and body, to facilitate the rapid and uniform setting of its tons of concrete as the building rose. Its bulk was cunningly subdivided by a web of infixed brick arches, not so much to distribute the loads and thrusts of an eventually compound structure as to check the warping flow of its inert material as it set. The whole exemplified the mobilization of a unique set of highly developed techniques to the sole end of supporting the shell of interior space.

In this mind and with this equipment, the architects of the age addressed themselves to the Empire's new requirements. The chief public business, the stated public festivals of the rank and file of the Empire, had been engrossed by appropriate rituals and appropriate spaces. The Empire also promoted leisure, besides well-being. It fixed a pattern of everyday life divided between business and recreation. As public leisure, it was a public concern, a province of imperial forethought. By tradition the common leisure had come to center itself around the ritual of the bath. It had come to involve not only cultivation of the body by exercise, bathing, and recreation but also cultivation of the mind by converse, reading, and attendance at displays of intellectual prowess. It was the dignity of this self-cultivation as a public institution with its own order, form, and pace that architecture now asserted and fixed grandly in a spatial environment of its own(Plates 70–75).

The basic program and requisites of the bathing establishment itself, without changing, had grown more exacting through refinement. The bath building, moreover, was now set in a complex of spaces devoted to the other uses of leisure —sports grounds, gardens, walks, lounges, lecture halls, libraries—each nobly framed as became its use, all united in a pervasive and compelling symmetry of design. The architectural kernel remained the bath. Resourceful architects sought in planning it to set up a progressive current of movement without retrogression or repetition. They sought to vary the shapes and sizes of volume in accord with economy of function and sensation and to exalt in great spaces the climactic moments of the experience. The solution that most widely approved itself over the Empire provided for twin vortexes of movement merging in a common stream, a doubled peripheral sequence of spaces converging on a central sequence. It conducted the bather from identical lobbies and dressing rooms at either side of the building, successively through identical pairs of three or more superheated baking and steaming rooms to a common hall of hot bathing, and thence through a tepid chamber or chambers to a common hall of cold bathing and swimming pool. The very nature of the design implied perfect bilateral symmetry, making the most compact and economical use of heated space for the benefit of large numbers.

An early version, executed at Lepcis Magna (Plates 70, 71), looks stiff and disjointed, clumsily served, as it was, by ground-level corridors. Yet its hall of cold bathing, cross-vaulted in three bays, was already an accomplished masterpiece of assured serenity, the first of a long line. Its sports ground was an un-related, if ingeniously contrived, appendage, whereas the classic example of the Baths of Caracalla at Rome was wedded to its garden setting (Plates 72, 73). There, the answering apsidal wings, which contained the lecture halls and lounges, counter-balanced the main building with complementary masses. At the back, the stadium, flanked by libraries, cupped the vista from the tier of hot rooms. The hot-bathing hall was a vast win-dowed rotunda, a tranquil eddy of light, which centered the movement it brought to a momentary halt; whereas the cold-bathing hall, with arrest, prompted dispersal by flights of vision down the long, axial enfilades. The whole was fashioned to marshal every man in a common and exhilarating rite of self-purification. Its civilizing power and universal hold on the peoples of the Empire was nowhere more forcefully displayed than in the great baths of Trier in Germany (Plates 74, 75). The invariable rules by which men were elevated in the human scale, the polite uses of ease were there laid down as in a primer of form. The expertly compact spatial composition, with its running counterpoint of cubical and spherical, dome and cross or barrel vault, gave compelling unity and urgency to the lesson.

The ordinary individual, whose life was the sum of the collective rituals of business and leisure, of street and square, theater and bath, was also a private individual. His identity and freedom were found and nourished in the benignant order of which he was a part. His status was guaranteed not by the laws and usages of the family, which once had bound him, but by the laws and usages of the Empire. It was the emperor who stood as father and lord to all mankind. The dwelling of the ordinary individual was no longer, even for public display, the matrix of the formal patterns of family life. Great or small, it was a retreat from the collective life, a haven of informal and anonymous privacy, empty of any significance but that of personal fancy or indulgence. It was informed by no common interest, had no necessary, common formal traits. All over the Empire men dwelt in such houses as they pleased or could afford, wherever they might be, in endless variety.

In the great cities, the metropolises of Rome, Antioch, and Alexandria, the massing of myriads of men, in reach of each other and of a center, provoked a special kind of domestic architecture, the multistoried tenement or apartment building. This, too, was a private architecture, unaffected by traditional or conventional exigencies, subject to control only as the state showed concern for such "housing" standards as safety and decency. As we meet this type of architecture in Rome or, more vividly, in Rome's image, its crowded port of Ostia, it was a fresh creation of the architects of the Empire (Plates 76, 77). They designed it with all the freedom that their adaptable materials and methods allowed them. They worked with ready inventiveness, in sweeping projects stated in terms of elementary functional and economic requirements—light, air, drainage, access by stairs, façades of shops, and offices behind arcades at street level. In blocks up to five or six stories high they combined quarters for every degree of the great middle class, from the stately, ground-floor town apartments of the well-to-do to the garret flats of the less favored. All above the lowest story were amply lighted and ventilated by windows.

Depending on the size and shape of the building lots, the apartments in any given block might be variously ranged around interior light wells, set one above another in compact piles or end to end in long strips above shops and arcades. These basic arrangements themselves might be combined and disposed as occasion demanded: great blocks with inner courtyards, straddling a community bathing establishment (Plate 80); light well and strip blocks joined about a garden; strip blocks connected to enframe a close with blocks of piled apartments in its midst. To the street each block presented rows of windows, and tiers of balconies (Plates 78, 79). Within, each apartment, of whatever size or plan, was spacious. The most modest consisted of living room, two bedrooms, kitchen, toilet, and passage, roomy and solidly enough built to be further subdivided by screen partitions. The common standard was the standard of comfort. Comfort and the casual collectivity of the multiple dwelling made personal privacy feasible. The window made it tolerable. From his window the individual looked down, detached, at the organized public life of his fellows, as seen in the frame of his temporary isolation.

The greatest individual of the Empire was the emperor, and his life was a life of state, from which there was only the illusion of escape. The spatial facsimile of the life of the emperor was the palace, an inner world, shaped to the imperial majesty and the imperial person. The palace as a deliberate, functional design was the work of the architecture of the High Empire. When it came into being on the Palatine hill in Rome toward the end of the first century of our era (Plate 81), it was conceived as the envelope both of the life of state and of the illusion of retreat from it. The life of state was a life of ceremony. The old, punctilious rituals of formal greeting, visiting, and dining had been solemnified about that being, the Emperor, who stood above all others. They were now courtly rituals of salutation, audience, and epiphany; the state apartments of the palace were made to contain them (Plates 82, 83).

The halls of audience and the state banqueting hall rose at opposite ends of a colonnaded formal garden. The halls of audience faced the ceremonial approach from the top of flights of stairs: a huge central hall, flanked by lesser halls. The three main spaces were majestic amplitudes, similar in shape, graduated in size and degree of illumination. The great throne hall, evenly flooded with light from front and back beneath its overarching vault, enveloped the suppliant in unhurried serenity from its threshold, gravely propelled him by its order of niches and columns toward the dais cupped by the shallow apse at the end of the room. The undivided whole that closed about him brought him near the lofty humanity and godlike condescension of one barely removed from the common ground. The lesser halls, one closed by a generous apse, the other by a terminal feature, in the same manner usher grandly in a single direction, while, in the disparity of their appointments, they reveal the hierarchy of precedence and protocol. The state banqueting hall similarly fixed the imperial presence in a shallow alcove beneath a wide curve of space, but there, strong front light and flickering side light, reflected from water, isolated it from the guests in their places before it. The hall was an immense and calmly focused square. It gave sideways, behind the banqueters, on garden courts that enframed elliptical fountains, in subtle contrast with the immobile majesty to which their eyes were drawn.

Alongside the state apartments lay the private apartments of the emperor and his suite. The approach to them through the formal garden was heralded by the dramatic reduction in scale of the wings that enclosed it. The pretense of escape from the ceremonious was enacted by their forms in a mannered, symmetrical play of curved and straight, open and closed, light and dark, on either side of an elegant octagonal pavilion. The same spatial preciosity pervaded the feigned informality of the private apartments (Plate 84). They were artfully secluded about a sunken garden, suites of capriciously formed, intimate cabinets, precisely disposed in stories. Their perfect etiquette was not less strict for being lively. They looked from windowed galleries at fixed prospects of the outside world, cunningly framed along the axes of the shallow arc of their façade (Plate 85).

41

The emperor, like the magnates of the Empire, might also seek relief from his public rôle and personality by withdrawal from the city. As the formal pattern of urban life and urban space had become more and more all-embracing, the villa had come to be less an instrument of the urbanization of the country than of divorce from urban constraints. By the relaxation of its strict, urban pattern of form it had come to reflect the slippered ease, the unfettered taste or caprice of an individual. Still obedient to the Roman feeling of the inherent order of sensation, the Roman will to control perception, it had become the means of disclosing a private ritual. The villa of the High Empire was a more or less loose and open aggregate of seemly and separate spaces, each fashioned for the enrichment of an individual life to the uses of the particular activity it enveloped. They were freely arranged in the landscape, with or without over-all symmetry, in the manner best calculated to take advantage of its qualities of terrain, exposure, and view. By park and garden the landscape was drawn into the complex of building and molded to form an organic part of a studied system of multiple spatial relations. The separate spaces, with their inner and outer enfilades and vistas, co-existed as the setting for the multiple aspects of an individual's refinement.

The villa built by the emperor Hadrian over a score of years (118–138 A.D.) below Tivoli, twenty miles from Rome, was the greatest of them all, an architectural portrait of the greatest individual of the Roman world (Plates 86, 87). Its sprawling fabric, flung impeccably over ridges and valleys, matched his every moment, mood, and attitude with a space to fit it. Morning, noon, or evening, moated (Plate 88) or towered solitude, free or formal society, repose, reflection, diversion, the prince, philosopher, poet, or poseur were alike caught in the villa's sensitive net. Each space, playfully or in earnest, laid down the rules of its moment—its manner, its measure, its nuance. Throughout the whole, as natural played against artificial form, supple mastery of structure and surface modeled the spaces with pliant variety and fantasy. The prevailing spheres and cylinders of space were convoluted. They flared and undulated (Plates 88a, 89). Light, water, and color denied the substantiality of their shells or gave form to insubstantial air (Plate 90).

Yet, for all its freedom, the emperor's whim and the emperor's architecture were bounded by the forms into which the Empire had crystallized all human experience. The villa might exhaust the vocabulary of forum and basilica, theater and bath, halls of state and privacy. It could not go beyond it. Its spaces enfolded, prompted, guided the individual to the same ends as the man in the street. The cosmos of the individual and the cosmos of society were at bottom one and the same. It was the same humane cosmos which the Empire had willed that men continue to make through the unfolding of ritual, to the end that man at last might be completely at home in the world. The only inhuman laws of this cosmos were the laws of nature. The only arbitrary power in it was the human power of the emperor, worshipful in so far as the natural order was manifested in him. On the one hand, this cosmos, for which man was beholden to none but himself, was his proudest creation, the monument of his supreme self-confidence. On the other, it was the measure of human frailty, of human inadequacy to support a burden of responsibility so crushing. It was the scene not only of man's proud self-reliance but of his frantic search for excuses, for the certitude he could not give himself. The imperial universe could be complete only because it denied realities inside and outside itself. It could be lasting only because it was built in ignorance of the pressures it would have to bear.

6 THE LATE EMPIRE

250–550 A.D.

The realities denied and the pressures ignored brought the Empire down in disorder, insecurity, and disillusion in the latter half of the third century. From then on its existence was a struggle to revive or to survive. Its outlook was narrowed, its remaining forces concentrated on the sole end of self-preservation. Of the old order, by which the scope of the Empire had been enlarged and its humanity deepened, only that could serve which might restore power and confidence or provide substitutes for them. The Late Empire would, when it might, build semblances of the old forms and the old grandeur, would declaim with brave but empty and anachronistic gestures, whistling in the dark. Such was the Basilica of Maxentius (Plate 91), a space lifted from the environment of public leisure to become the last, pagan place of public business in Rome. The true shape of a new order was the shape of such contemporary buildings as the pleasure dome in the Licinian Gardens, known as the temple of Minerva Medica (Plate 91a). It was eloquent of the constriction of the Empire's scope, the dissipation of its humanity in the effort to save it, the mirage of unearthly bliss. A squat, polygonal tower, impregnably girt with buttressing apses and piers, encapsulated an airy pavilion, whose tall curtains, dissolved by light and movement, melting insensibly into the circle of its dome, were scarcely to be grasped as an enclosure. At eye level they billowed outward in an uninterrupted kaleidoscope of apses and garden vistas. The drum high above was an immaterial ring of light beneath a shimmering canopy of mosaic. All below was uncertainly shifting. All above was radiance, a remotely ethereal promise. Only those practices and spaces had power that might summon strength or its appearance, or evoke past and future promise. These, the institutions of authority and worship, the rituals of state and church, had both real and symbolic import as never before. The imperial house was the real source of earthly power and security, the symbol of earthly hope and assurance. The church was the sole source of consolation in this world, the symbol of security deferred, of hope transferred to the next.

The Empire and its architecture died hard. In a permanent state of defense, its towns now strongpoints, walled in from each other and the hinterland, divided, dismembered, it endured for three more centuries. It did not cease to be Roman until the faith in man's power to make his own destiny and to legislate the ways of God had left it. Over these years the public person of the emperor was ever more stiffly clothed in ritual, ever more shrunk into an armor of ceremony that made him the effigy of the power of the Empire at bay. The generous spaces of the old palace in Rome were ill-suited to these hieratic patterns. The palace of the new Rome in the East, Constantinople, was cast in a different mold. But the proper place of the emperor in these years was nearer the front, in Trier, Milan, Ravenna, Sirmium, Nicomedia, Antioch. In each of these the imperial

45

presence and the imperial state engendered a palace. The prototype was the palace near Salona in Dalmatia, whence the emperor Diocletian ruled his half of the Empire for a few years at the beginning of the fourth century (Plates 92, 92a, 93).

It wore the aspect of a fortress, a permanent Roman camp, of which the palace proper was the headquarters building. What would have been the principal street of the cantonment was an axial, processional way. Its colonnades ended in taller screen arcades, which framed a shadow-barred ceremonial court before the porch of entrance to the presence or of its public apparition. Within, the elemental spaces of the old palace were compressed into a compact block and stiffened to an intricate, liturgical pattern. Each separate space was re-designed to have a single, ostentatious force, which was heavy and emphatic. Beyond porch and portal a circular antechamber, like a lock of suspense, withheld attention until it was projected down the narrow length of the throne hall toward the back-lighted presence at the farther end. A basilical hall of audience to one side, brought to focus on a deep apse, was balanced on the other by the domed, massively profiled banqueting hall of state. The private apartments filled either end of the composition.

The villa, again, to which emperor or high officer of the Empire might repair, bore the nervous imprint of his private insecurity, of a leisure apprehensively enjoyed. The great villa of Piazza Armerina in Sicily (Plates 94, 95) was, as it were, a villa of the High Empire shrunk together and distorted. It huddled in the landscape but ignored it, deliberately excluding nature to turn inward on itself. This introspective world, reduced in scope and variety, was inwardly fractioned and abruptly disjointed, and outwardly amorphous. Its members were proliferously oblivious of their outline or mass, as though they had been blindly dug out of the body of space. Inorganically juxtaposed, each with its private mode and formal symmetry, they were strung together by an overlay of lines of sight, contrived directives, which were aimed at intrusive visual objectives. The individual spaces themselves were restlessly and incisively convoluted, drawn out in appendages, and apsidal extensions, which absorbed the central volumes. The traditional spaces of pomp and refinement—monumental portal, formal garden, halls of audience and retreat, banquet hall, bath—recurred as in a nightmare.

It was the Church that challenged the architects of the Late Empire to their boldest achievements. The new religion had become a public institution overnight. Its manner and places of worship were as different from the old as its God was different from the old symbols of immanent power. The new rites were congregational rites performed indoors. They assembled worshipers in a building and directed their attention to the sacrificial mystery enacted at the altar or to the homilies of a priestly orator. For the Christian community the religious meeting took the place of the old forms of secular gathering. The architects of the Late Empire surrounded it with the old forms of secular space. Forms designed to urge mind and sense in a single direction were ready to hand in the basilica and the palatial halls of audience, forms designed to hold them in a centered suspension in banquet halls and baths. Both were forms that architects were also reshaping about the rituals of the palace.

In the basilical church (Plates 96, 97) the old secular basilica of passive volume and circumambient counterflow and eddy was turned into a single tide of space, as irresistible as that of the Old Roman temple space. Aisles and nave now swept side by side to a single conclusion. All the old devices for directing space—the measured pace of columns, the trajectory of horizontals, the side-lighted tunnel of space, the enframing arch, the terminal apse—were brought into play. They combined to grip the worshiper in a singleness of intent, scarcely deflected by the feeble crosscurrent that might be set up by a pulpit advanced on one side of the nave. In the church of central plan (Plates 98, 99), domed polyhedron or rotunda, men were massed in a pool of space, magnetized by the altar which drew them to face it. The space was radial about this dominant diameter, and the architects of the Late Empire ringed its luminous core

47

with a deep penumbra. In so doing, they constricted the center to a well beneath its dome, which was lifted on a drum; they scalloped its confines nervously with galleries, and drew off its volume into the aisle and extended apse. The serene humanity of the old order was dispersed in tensions. Man at the bottom of the shaft of transcendent truth was hedged by shadows.

The rituals and spaces of palace and church were what was left when the Western world ceased to be Roman. At the final moment of this passing, defying three centuries of the past and ten centuries of the future, Roman architecture made a last, anachronistic assertion of Roman values (Plate 100). Holy Wisdom was a goddess the High Empire might well have worshiped. Justinian's great church was a space that Hadrian might well have been at home in, an iridescent whole of unruffled composure and comprehensibility. Its tripartite totality was centered on man. The great circles of its firmament described his course, exalting him and returning him to earth. Its arcaded length plotted the finite direction. Its apses rounded its completion. Hagia Sophia spoke to the Middle Ages of a world they had lost. It awed them with a fullness and finality of life they could neither comprehend nor experience, a fullness and finality of form they could not repeat.

Rome, September 1960

48

1. Hut of the Palatine Village, 8th century B.C.

2. *The Regia in the Roman* **Forum**, *6th–1st centuries B.C.*

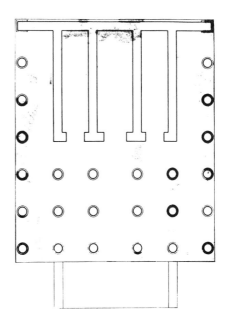

3. *The Capitolium, Rome, 6th–1st centuries B.C.*

4. *The Temple of Minerva, Veii, 5th century B.C.*

5. *The Temples of the Arx, Cosa, 3rd–2nd centuries B.C.*

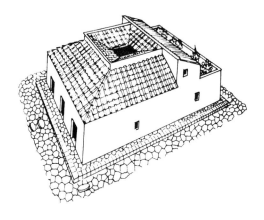

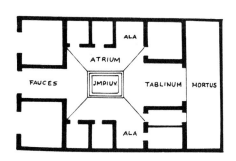

6. *A typical old Roman house, 4th–3rd centuries B.C.*

7. *The Atrium of the House of the Surgeon, Pompeii, 3rd century B.C.*

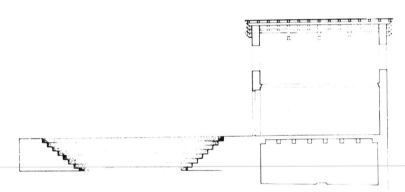

8. *The Comitium and Curia, Cosa, 3rd century B.C.*

9. *The Atrium Publicum, Cosa, 3rd century B.C.*

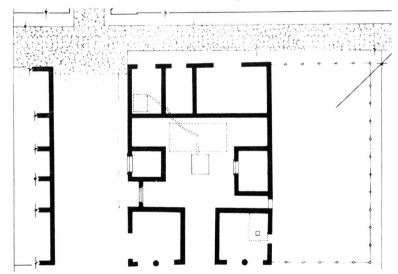

10. *The wall and a gate, Falerii, 3rd century B.C.*

11. *A gate, Norba, 4th century B.C.*

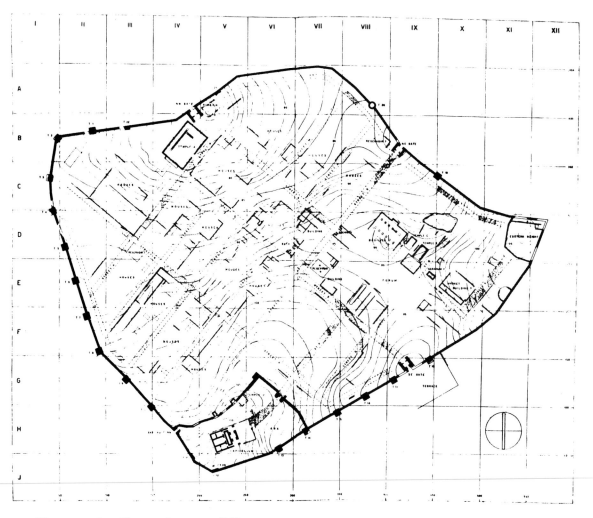

12. *The town plan, Cosa, 3rd century B.C.*

14. *The Porticus of Metellus, Rome, 2nd century B.C.*

13. *The Temple of Hercules, Cori, 2nd century B.C.*

15. The Temple of Apollo, Pompeii, 1st century B.C.

16. *The Temple platform, Terracina, 2nd century B.C.*

17. *The Round Temple, Tivoli, 1st century B.C.*

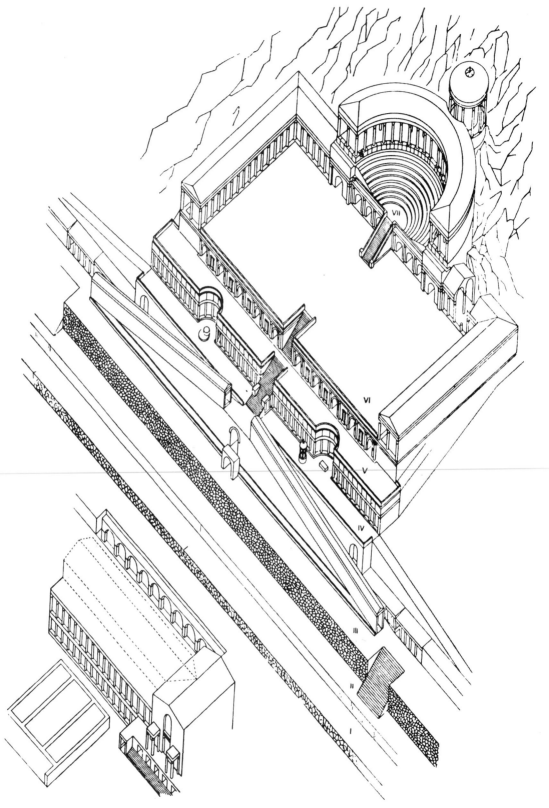

18. *The Sanctuary of Fortuna, Praeneste, 2nd century B.C.*

19. *The Sanctuary of Fortuna, Praeneste.*

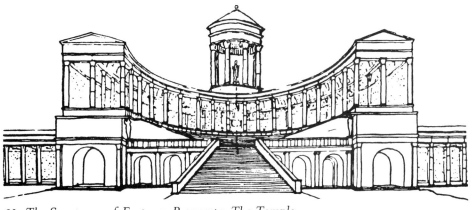

20. *The Sanctuary of Fortuna, Praeneste. The Temple.*

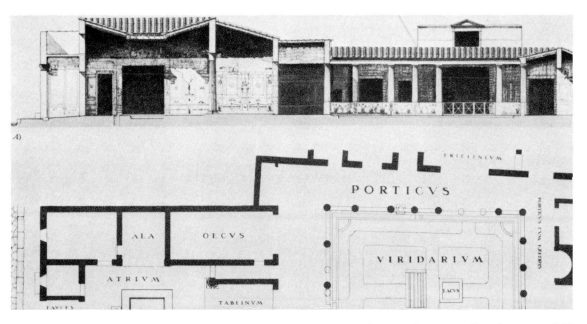

21. *The House of Menander, Pompeii, 2nd century B.C.*

23. *The Peristyle Garden of the House of the Vettii, Pompeii, 2nd century B.C.*

22. *The Atrium of the House of Menander.*

24. *The House of the Silver Wedding, Pompeii, 2nd century B.C. A dining alcove.*

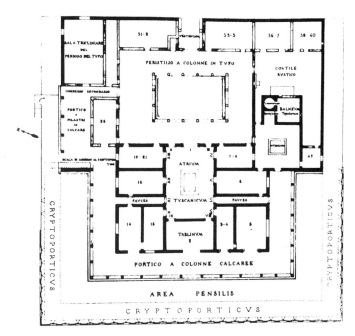

25. *The Villa of the Mysteries, near Pompeii, 2nd century B.C.*

26. *The Villa of the Mysteries.*

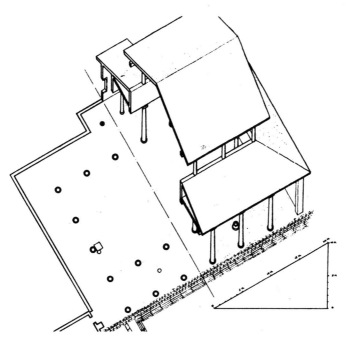

27. *The Basilica, Cosa, 2nd century B.C.*

28. *The Basilica, Cosa.*

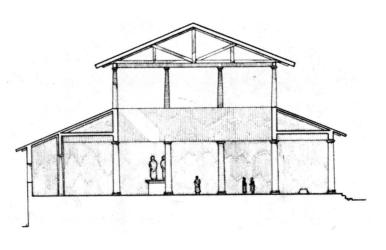

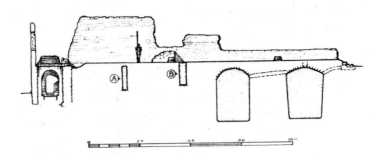

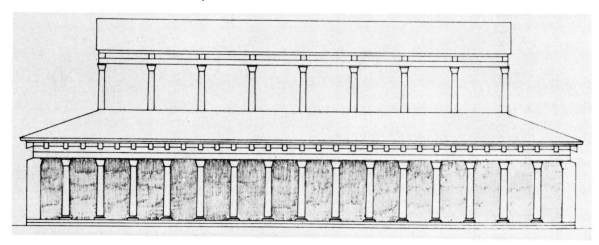

29. *The Basilica, Ardea, 2nd century B.C.*

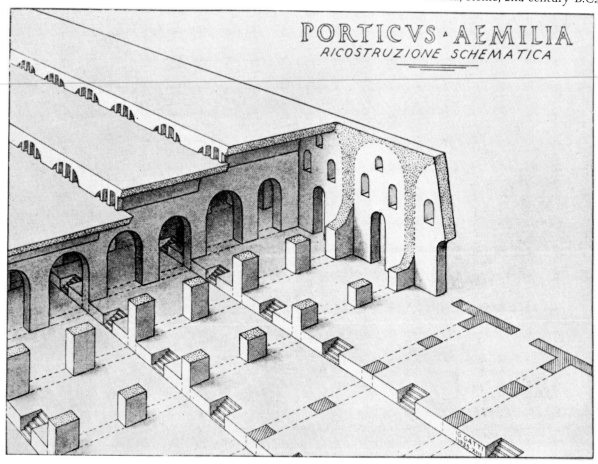

30. *The Porticus Aemilia, Rome, 2nd century B.C.*

PORTICVS · AEMILIA
RICOSTRUZIONE SCHEMATICA

31. *The Porticus Aemilia.*

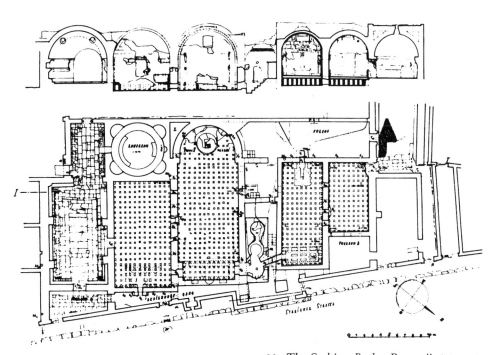

32. *The Stabian Baths, Pompeii, 1st century B.C.*

33. *The Caldarium, Forum Baths, Pompeii, 1st century B.C.*

34. The Maison Carrée, Nîmes, France, 1st century B.C.

35. The Forum of Caesar, Rome, 1st century B.C.

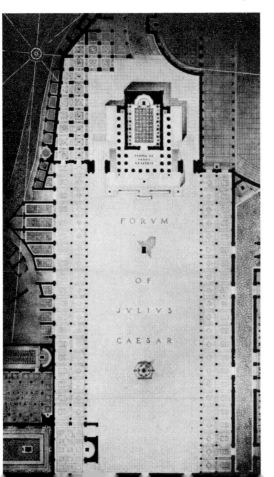

36. *The Forum of Caesar.*

37. *The Forum of Augustus, Rome, 1st century A.D.*

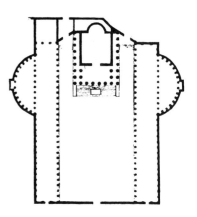

38. *The Forum of Augustus.*

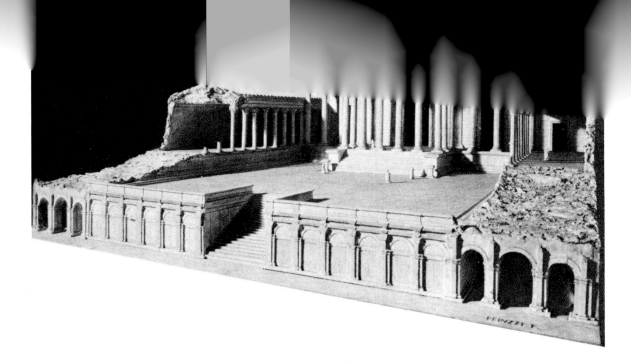

39. *The Capitolium and Forum, Brescia, 1st century A.D.*

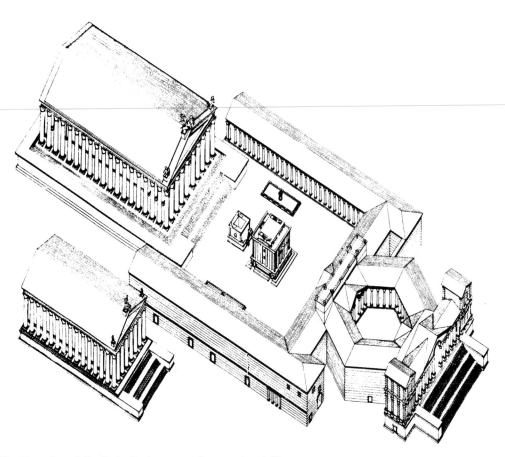

40. *The Temples of Baalbek, Syria, 1st–2nd centuries A.D.*

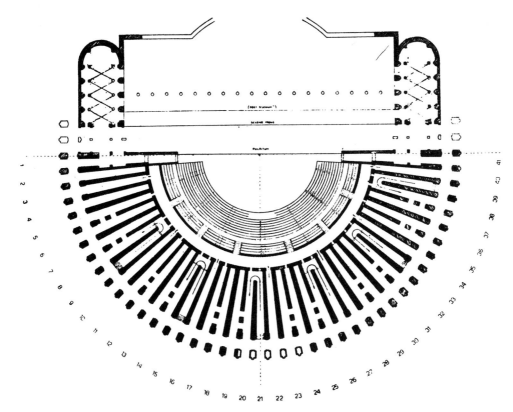

41. *The Theater of Marcellus, Rome, 1st century B.C.*

42. *The Theater of Marcellus.*

43. *The Theater of Marcellus.*

44. *The Theater, Orange, France, 1st century B.C.*

45. *The Theater, Sabratha, Tripolitania, 2nd century A.D.*

46. *The Amphitheater, Verona, 1st century A.D.*

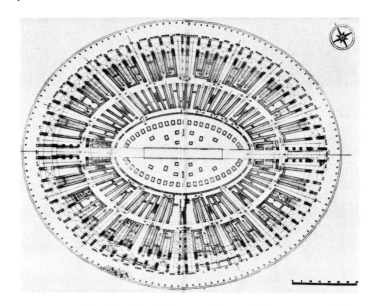

47. *The Amphitheater, Pozzuoli, 1st century A.D.*

48. *The Colosseum, Rome, 1st century A.D.*

49. *The Colosseum.*

50. *The Circus Maximus, Rome, 1st–3rd centuries A.D.*

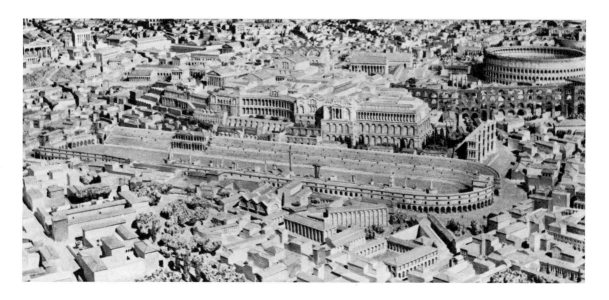

51. *The Hippodrome of Gerasa, Jordan, 1st century A.D.*

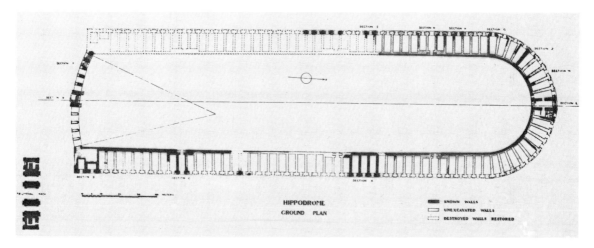

HIPPODROME
GROUND PLAN

KNOWN WALLS
UNEXCAVATED WALLS
DESTROYED WALLS RESTORED

53. *Colonnaded street and arch, Timgad, Algeria, 2nd century A.D.*

54. *Colonnaded street, Apamea, Syria, 2nd century A.D.*

52. *The Circus of Maxentius, near Rome, 4th century A.D.*

55. *The Monumental Arch, Susa, 1st century B.C.*

56. *Centuriated farmland around a Roman town, 1st century A.D.*

57. *The Claudian Aqueduct, near Rome, 1st century A.D.*

58. *The Via Flaminia, north of Rome.*

59. *Roadcutting in the Alpine passes.*

60. Pont du Gard, viaduct and aqueduct near Nîmes, France, 1st century A.D.

61. The Forum of Trajan, Rome, 2nd century A.D.

62. *The Forum of Trajan, Basilica Ulpia.*

63. *The Forum of Augusta Raurica, Switzerland, 2nd century A.D.*

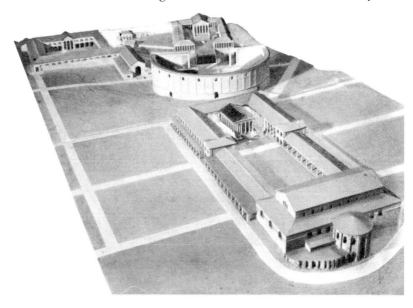

64. The Severan Forum, Lepcis Magna, Tripolitania, 3rd century A.D.

65. The Pantheon, Rome, 2nd century A.D.

66. The Pantheon. Façade.

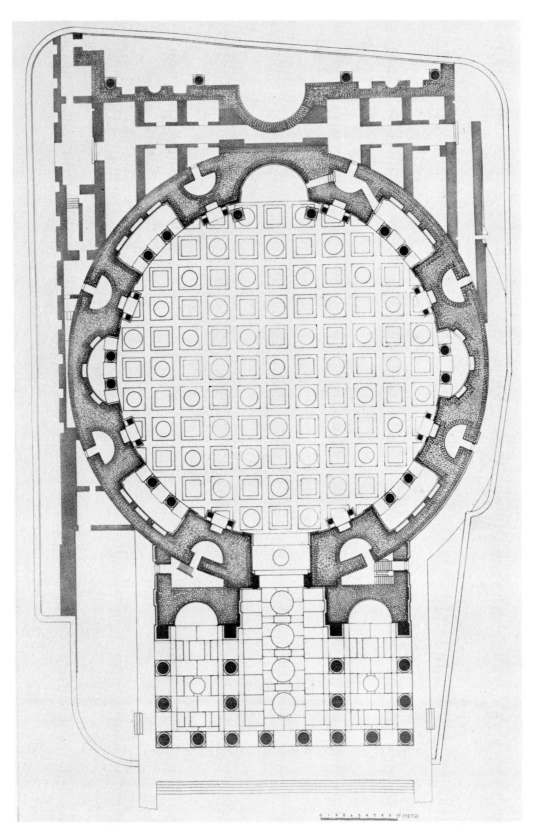

67. *The Pantheon. Plan.*

68. The Pantheon. Interior.

69. *The Pantheon. Structure.*

70. *Baths, Lepcis Magna, Tripolitania, 2nd century A.D.*

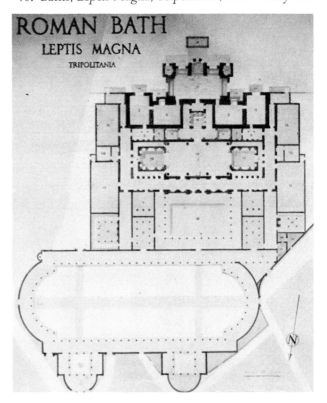

71. *Baths, Lepcis Magna. Interior.*

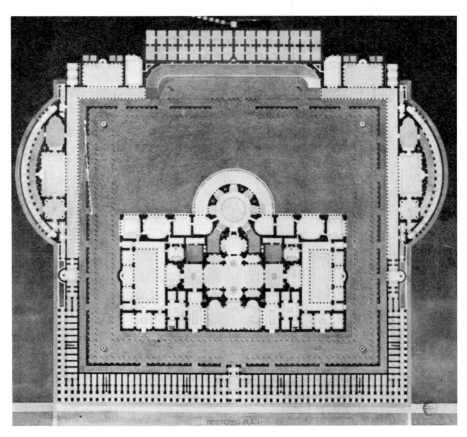

72. *The Baths of Caracalla, Rome, 3rd century A.D.*

73. *The Baths of Caracalla.*

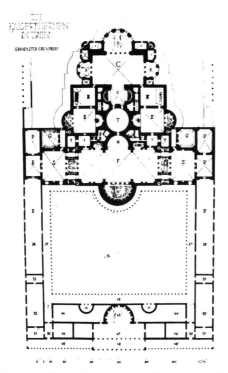

74. *The Imperial Baths, Trier, Germany, 3rd century A.D.*

75. *The Imperial Baths. Interior.*

76. *Apartment blocks, Rome, 2nd–3rd centuries A.D.*

77. *Apartment blocks, Ostia, 2nd–3rd centuries A.D.*

78. *Apartment blocks, Ostia.*

79. *Apartment blocks, Ostia.*

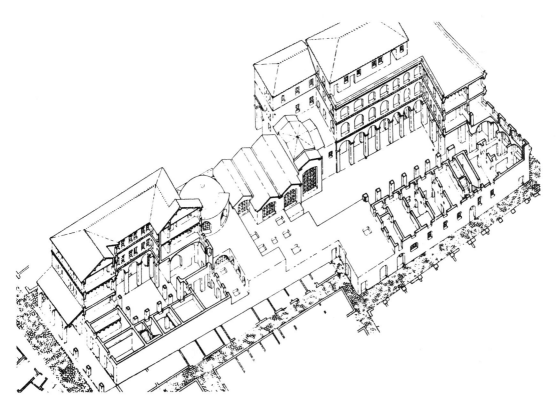

80. Apartment blocks, Ostia.

81. The Imperial Palace, Rome, 1st–3rd centuries A.D.

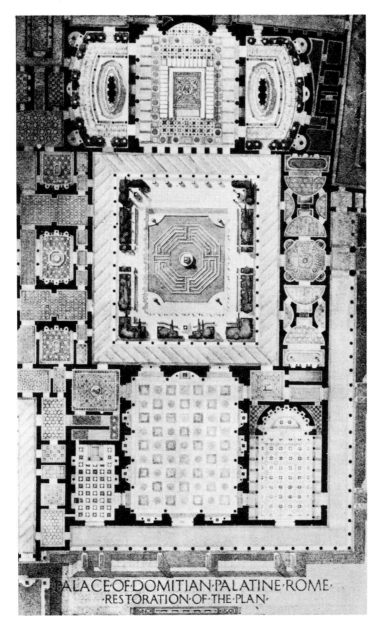

82. The Imperial Palace. State Apartments.

83. The Imperial Palace. State Apartments.

84. *The Imperial Palace. Private Apartments.*

85. The Imperial Palace. Private Apartments.

86. Hadrian's Villa, near Tivoli, 2nd century A.D.

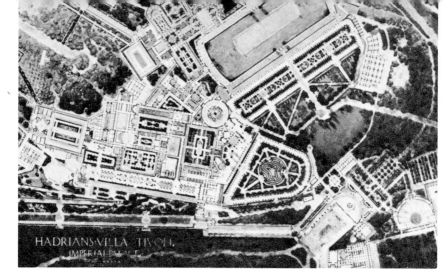

87. Hadrian's Villa. Central part.

88. Hadrian's Villa. Circular Casino.

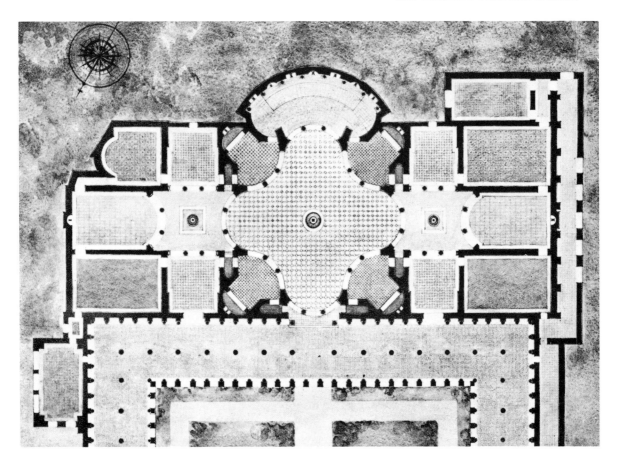

88a. *Hadrian's Villa. Hall of State.*

89. *Hadrian's Villa. Hall of State.*

90. *Hadrian's Villa. Dining Pavilion.*

91. The Basilica of Maxentius, Rome, 4th century A.D.

91a. A kiosk in the Licinian Gardens, Rome, 4th century A.D.

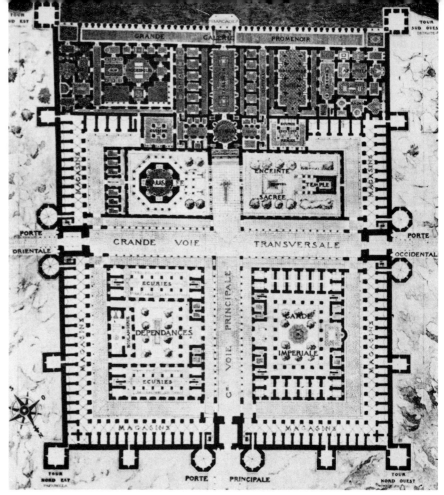

92. The Palace of Diocletian, Spalato, 4th century A.D.

92a. The Palace of Diocletian.

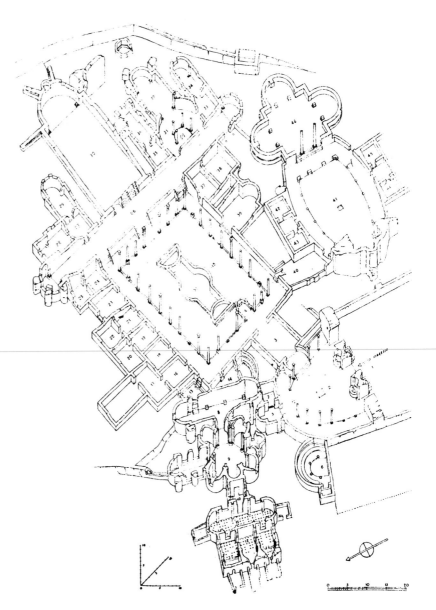

94. The Villa, Piazza Armerina, 4th century A.D.

95. *The Villa, Piazza Armerina.*

96. *The Church of Santa Maria Maggiore, Rome, 5th century A.D.*

97. *The Church of Santa Sabina, Rome, 5th century A.D.*

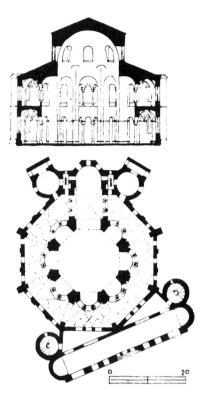

98. *The Church of San Vitale, Ravenna, 6th century A.D.*

99. *The Church of San Vitale. Interior.*

100. The Church of Hagia Sophia, Constantinople, 6th century A.D.

SELECTED BIBLIOGRAPHY

GENERAL

ANDERSON, W. J., SPIERS, R. P., and ASHBY, T. *The Architecture of Ancient Rome*. London, 1927.

BLAKE, M. P. *Ancient Roman Construction in Italy from the Prehistoric Period to Augustus*. Washington, 1947.
Roman Construction in Italy from Tiberius through the Flavians. Washington, 1959.

CREMA, L. *L'architettura romana*. Turin, 1959.

DURM, J. *Die Baukunst der Etrusker. Die Baukunst der Römer*. Stuttgart, 1905.

LUGLI, G. *La tecnica edilizia romana*. Rome, 1957.

LUNDBERG, E. *Arkitekturens Formspråk*. Vol. 2. Stockholm, 1951.

RIVOIRA, G. T. *Roman Architecture*. Oxford, 1925.

ROBERTSON, D. S. *A Handbook of Greek and Roman Architecture*. Cambridge, 1954.

VITRUVIUS. *De Architectura Libri Decem*.

CHAPTER 1

BRYAN, W. R. *Italic Hut Urns*. ("Papers and Monographs of the American Academy in Rome," Vol. 4.) Rome, 1925.

DAVICO, A. *Ricostruzione probabile dell'abitazione laziale del primo periodo del ferro*. ("Monumenti Antichi," Vol. 41.) Rome, 1951.

DE FRANCISCI, P. *Primordia civitatis*. Rome, 1959.

GJERSTAD, E. *Early Rome*, Pts. I, II. ("Skrifter utgivna av Svenska Institutet i Rom," 4°, Vol. 17.) Lund, 1953–1956.

LATTE, K. *Römische Religionsgeschichte*. ("Handbuch der Altertumswissenschaft," Vol. V, No. 1.) Munich, 1960.

NORDEN, E. *Aus altrömischen Priesterbüchern*. Lund, 1939.

CHAPTER 2

ANDRÉN, A. *Architectural Terracottas from Etrusco–Italic Temples*. ("Skrifter utgivna av Svenska Institutet i Rom" 4°, Vol. 6.) Lund and Leipzig, 1939–1940.

AVORIO, M. *L'evoluzione dell'atrio nella casa pompeiana*. Naples, 1935.

BROWN, F. E. *Cosa I*. ("Memoirs of the American Academy in Rome," Vol. 20.) Rome, 1951.

Cosa II, Part I. ("Memoirs of the American Academy in Rome," Vol. 26.) Rome, 1960.

The Regia. ("Memoirs of the American Academy in Rome," Vol. 12.) Rome, 1935.

CASTAGNOLI, F. *Ippodamo di Mileto e l'urbanistica a pianta ortagonale*. Rome, 1956.

GJERSTAD, E. *Early Rome*, op. cit.

"Etruskerna och Rom," in *San Giovenale. Etruskerna landet och folket*. Malmö, 1960.

LAKE, A. K. "The Origin of the Roman House," *American Journal of Archaeology*, Vol. 41, 1937.

114

PATRONI, G. *Architettura preistorica–Architettura etrusca.* Bergamo, 1941.

RICHARDSON, L. "Cosa and Rome: Curia and Comitium," *Archaeology.* Vol. 10, 1957.

STEFANI, E. *Scavi archeologici a Veio in contrada Piazza d'Armi.* ("Monumenti Antichi," Vol. 40.) Rome, 1944.

WARD PERKINS, J. B. "Early Roman Towns in Italy," *Town Planning Review,* Vol. 26, 1955.

WELIN, E. *Atrium Publicum.* ("Studien zur Topographie des Forum Romanum.") Lund, 1953.

CHAPTER 3

BOETHIUS, A. "The Hellenized Italic Town and its Legacy to Imperial Rome," *The Golden House of Nero.* Ann Arbor, 1960. "Die spätrepublikanischen Warenhaüser in Ferentino und Tivoli," *Acta Archaeologica,* Vol. 3, 1932.

CARRINGTON, R. C. "Some Ancient Italian Country-Houses," *Antiquity,* Vol. 8, 1934.

DE 'ANGELIS D'OSSAT, G. *Tecnica costrutiva e impianti delle terme.* Rome, 1943.

DELBRÜCK, R. *Hellenistische Bauten in Latium.* Strassburg, 1907–1912.

DE SANCTIS, G. "Vita e pensiero nell'età delle grandi conquiste," *Storia dei Romani,* Vol. IV, No. 1, Pt. 2, Florence, 1953.

DRERUP, H. *Bildraum und Realraum in der römischen Architektur.* ("Mitteilungen des Deutschen Archaeologischen Instituts, Römische Abteilung," Vol. 66.) Heidelberg, 1959. "Die römische Villa," *Marburger Winckelmann-Program.* Marburg, 1959.

FASOLO, F., and GULLINI, G. *Il tempio della Fortuna Primigenia a Palestrina.* Rome, 1953.

GATTI, G. "*Saepta Iulia*" e "*Porticus Aemilia*" *nella* "*Forma*" *severiana.* ("Bullettino della Commissione Archeologica Comunale di Roma," Vol. 52.) Rome, 1934.

GRIMAL, P. *Le siècle des Scipions.* Paris, 1953.

GULLINI, G. "I monumenti dell'acropoli di Ferentino," *Archeologica Classica.* Vol. 6, 1954.

KÄHLER, H. *Das Fortunaheiligtum von Palestrina Praeneste.* Saarbrücken, 1958.

KRENCKER, D. *Die Trierer Kaiserthermen.* Augsburg, 1929.

MAIURI, A. "Portico e peristilio," *Parola del Passato,* Vol. 1, 1946.

WARD PERKINS, J. B. *Constantine and the Origins of the Christian Basilica.* ("Papers of the British School in Rome," No. 22.) London, 1954.

WELIN, E. *Die Basilika als Gerichts- und Amtslokal.* ("Studien zur Topographie des Forum Romanum.") Lund, 1953.

CHAPTER 4

BIEBER, M. *History of the Greek and Roman Theater.* Princeton, 1939.

DREXEL, F. "Gebaüde für die öffentlichen Schauspiele in Italien und den Provinzen," in L. Friedlander, *Darstellungen aus der Sittengeschichte Roms,* Vol. IV. Leipzig, 1921.

GJERSTAD, E. "Die Ursprungsgeschichte der römischen Kaiserfora," *Opuscula Archaeologica,* Vol. 3. Lund, 1944.

HANSON, J. A. *Roman Theater-temples.* Princeton, 1959.

THOMSEN, R. "Studien über den ursprünglichen Bau des Caesarforums," *Opuscula Archaeologica,* Vol. 2. Lund, 1941.

CHAPTER 5

BARTOLI, A. *Domus Augustana.* Rome, 1938.

BELTRAMI, L. *Il Pantheon.* Milan, 1898.

BETTINI, S. *L'architettura di San Marco.* Padua, 1946.

BOETHIUS, A. "The Domestic Architecture of the Imperial Age," *The Golden House of Nero.* Ann Arbor, 1960.

CALZA, G. *Scavi di Ostia,* Vol. 1. Rome, 1953.

CLARK, E. *Rome and a Villa.* Garden City, 1952.

HANSEN, E. *La "Piazza d'Oro" e la sua cupola.* Copenhagen, 1960.

KÄHLER, H. *Hadrian und seine Villa bei Tivoli.* Berlin, 1950.

KRENCKER, D. *Die Trierer Kaiserthermen.* Augsburg, 1929.

LUGLI, G. *Roma Antica, Il centro monumentale.* Rome, 1946.

MEIGGS, R. *Roman Ostia.* Oxford, 1960.

RODENWALDT, G. "Römische Staatsarchitektur," in H. Berve, *Das neue Bild der Antike*, Vol. 2. Leipzig, 1942.

SWOBODA, K. M. *Römische und romanische Paläste*. Vienna, 1924.

VIGHI, R. *The Pantheon*. Translated by J. B. Ward Perkins. Rome, 1957.

CHAPTER 6

BOVINI, G. *San Vitale di Ravenna*. Milan, 1955.

BULIC, F. *Kaiser Diokletians Palast in Split*. Zagreb, 1929.

DEICHMANN, F. W. *Frühchristliche Bauten und Mosaiken von Ravenna*. Baden-Baden, 1958.

DYGGVE, E. *Ravennatum Palatium Sacrum*. Copenhagen, 1941. *Aula Sacra-Aula Sanctum*. Copenhagen, 1959.

GENTILI, G. V. *La villa Erculia di Piazza Armerina*. Rome, 1959.

GRABAR, A. *Martyrium*. Paris, 1946.

NEUERBERG, N. "Some Considerations on the Architecture of the Imperial Villa at Piazza Armerina," *Marsyas*, Vol. 8, 1959.

PACE, B. *I mosaici di Piazza Armerina*. Rome, 1955.

ZALOZIECKY, W. R. *Die Sophienkirche in Konstantinopel*. Rome–Freiburg, 1936.

INDEX

Numbers in regular roman type refer to text pages; *italic* figures refer to the plates.

SOURCES OF ILLUSTRATIONS

A. Accrocca, *Cori* (Rome, 1933): 13

Alinari: 11, 17, 23, 26, 42, 79, 86, 91a, 92a, 96, 97

American Academy in Rome: 8, 9, 27, 28, 29, 35, 36, 70, 71, 72, 82, 83, 87, 88a, 89

Anderson: 24

Wayne Andrews: 34

Architettura e Arti Decorative, vol. 2, 1922-23: 48

L. Beltrami, *Il Pantheon* (Milan, 1898): 69

British School in Rome: 64

Brogi: 33

Bulletino Centro Studi St. dell'Architettura, vol. 7, 1953: 41

Bulletino della Commissione Archeologica Comunale di Roma, vol. 52, 1934: 30

L. Canina, *Gli edifizi di Roma antica*, vol. 3 (Rome, 1848): 62

Cappabianca (after Luckenbach): 6

G. Caputo, *Il teatro di Sabratha* (Rome, 1959): 45

P. Collart and P. Coupel, *L'autel monumental de Baalbek* (Paris, 1951): 40

Deutsches Archaeologisches Institut-Rom: 22, 99

A. Di Giovanni: 50, 81

Fototeca Unione: 2, 10, 14, 15, 16, 19, 31, 38, 43, 46, 49, 52, 53, 55, 57, 58, 59, 66, 68, 78, 88, 95

Gabinetto Fotografico Nazionale: 84, 85

E. Hebrard, *Spalato* (Paris, 1912): 92

Hirmer Verlag: 100

Historisches Museum, Basel, Switzerland: 63

Istituto di Etruscologia, Università di Roma : 4

H. Kähler, *Das Fortunaheiligtum von Palestrina Praeneste* (Saarbrücken, 1958): 18, 20

C. H. Kraeling, *Gerasa* (New Haven, 1938): 51

D. Krencker, *Die Trierer Kaiserthermen* (Augsburg, 1929): 74, 75

La Pianta Marmorea di Roma (Rome, 1960): 76

L'architettura antica in Dalmazia (Turin, n.d.): 93

E. Lundberg, *Arkitekturens Formspråk* (Stockholm, 1951): 37, 98

A. Maiuri, *La Casa del Menandro* (Rome, 1933): 21; *La Villa dei Misteri* (Rome, 1931): 25; *Studi e ricerche sull'anfiteatro flavio puteolano* (Naples, 1955): 47

Memoirs of the American Academy in Rome, vol. 6, 1927: 90; vol. 20, 1951: 12; vol. 26, 1960: 5

Musei Comunali, Rome: 39, 54, 60, 61, 65, 73

N. D. Phot.: 44

B. Pace, *I mosaici di Piazza Armerina* (Rome, 1955): 94

Palladio, vol. 5, 1941: 80

Papers of the British School in Rome, vol. 12, 1932: 91

San Giovenale (Malmö, 1960): 3, 4

Scavi di Ostia, vol. 1 (Rome, 1953): 77

G. Schween, *Die Beheizungsanlage der stabianer Thermen in Pompeii* (Hamburg, 1938): 32

Sopritendenza ai Monumenti del Lazio: 67

Sopritendenza Foro Romano e Palatino: 1

United States Army Air Force: 56

Courtesy Tatiana Warscher: 7